HOW TO SURVIVE AS A

Child Welfare Social Worker

MICHAELLA CONTEH

How to Survive as a Child Welfare Social Worker

Copyright © 2021

Michaella Conteh

All Rights Reserved.

No portion of this publication may be reproduced, stored in an electronic system, or transmitted in any form or by any means (electronic, mechanical, photocopy, recording, or otherwise) without written permission from the author. Brief quotations may be used in literary reviews.

Paperback ISBN 13: 978-1-7373683-1-1

eBook ISBN 13: 978-1-7373683-0-4

This work is for informational purposes only. Every attempt has been made to verify the accuracy of the information at the time of publication. The author will not be held liable or claim accountability for any loss or injuries. Use, view, and implement the strategies contained herein at your own risk. The author disclaims any responsibility for the inaccuracy of the content, including but not limited to errors or omissions.

For information and bulk ordering, contact:

Michaella Conteh

contehmmc@outlook.com

Dedication

This book is dedicated to my Social Worker colleagues and friends who are working tirelessly in the field to ensure the children are safe and that the families receive the best support while working alongside the Child Welfare System.

This book is also dedicated to those aspiring to become a Social Worker in the Child Welfare field.

CONTENTS

Introduction 1

Chapter 1: What is Child Welfare? 5

    Family Reunification 6

    Family Maintenance 8

    Permanent Planning 12

    Legal Guardianship 13

    Adoption 14

    Non-Minor Dependent 16

Chapter 2: Types of Jobs as a Child Welfare Social Worker 27

    Child Abuse and Neglect Call Center 27

    Emergency Response 30

    Dependency Investigation / Court Unit 32

    Family Reunification, Family Maintenance, or Permanency Planning/Continuing Unit 36

    Adoption Department 40

    Placement Department 42

    Resource Family Approval Unit 43

Chapter 3: Organization 45

Chapter 4: Resources in Child Welfare 53

Chapter 5: 10 Tips to Survive as a Child Welfare Social Worker . 59

In Closing… 63

Child Welfare Social Worker Chart 64

About the Author 65

Introduction

*C*hild *Welfare Social Worker* is a title typically applied to Child Protective Services (CPS) professionals. A Child Welfare Social Worker protects children from abuse and neglect or removes children from high-risk homes where they have experienced severe neglect or physical, sexual, or emotional abuse. To be very clear: Child Welfare Social Workers do not remove children because they are "poor" or "do not have housing."

As a Child Welfare Social Worker, there have been instances where the families are homeless, going from one hotel to another, and so on. Homelessness is not a reason to remove children. Conversely, if there are concerns about drug use around the children or children being left alone for days without adult supervision, CPS will protect the children. That is especially notable because I have often encountered people who have asked, "Why can't CPS give that money to the parents who are poor rather than give it to foster parents?"

As a Child Welfare Social Worker, you will be tasked with constantly assisting children and their families by:

- Resolving conflicts.
- Conducting ongoing assessments.
- Working with various service providers within the community.
- Working with the whole family unit.
- Providing the best resources for the children, youth, and families.

My reason for writing this book is that I have observed how many Social Workers who start working for CPS are not provided with a guide detailing what to expect as a Child Welfare Social Worker. Yes, you "learn about" social work when you attend undergrad or grad school. However, the reality of the work is often hidden and not discussed.

I desire to provide Social Workers who are considering entering the Child Welfare field to know what to expect, have a useful guide to reference, and to hear from someone in the field for about six years while working at different programs and working for the county. This book will provide insight into what Child Welfare is, along with the pros and cons of Child Welfare Social Workers. Demonstrated within, you will read about:

- The different services the families go through within the Child Welfare system.
- The various departments you can work in as a Child Welfare Social Worker.
- The pros and cons of working within each department.
- Staying organized as you juggle high caseloads.
- Considering providing resources to families.
- Self-care tips on how you can survive as a Child Welfare Social Worker.

I must be frank here and say it is always best to work on yourself and any past traumas before beginning this career. Being a Child Welfare Social Worker is not an easy job, as it brings many personal emotions to the forefront. I hope that this book will be a helpful tool and an excellent resource for all current and up-and-coming Social Workers.

CHAPTER 1

What is Child Welfare?

As a Child Protective Services (CPS) representative, you—the Social Worker—ensure children and youth are safe in their living environment. As a Child Welfare Social Worker, the number one thing you consistently think about is SAFETY. In each instance you encounter, ask yourself, "If I leave this place right now, will these children be okay with this adult or living condition?"

Another thing about safety is constantly consulting with your supervisor or management before making any decision. One thing I have learned in this field is to always, always, ALWAYS consult.

As a Child Welfare Social Worker, you must learn the differences and purposes for each of the following programs:

- Family Reunification
- Family Maintenance

- Permanent Planning
- Legal Guardianship
- Adoption

Some children go through each of those processes, especially if they enter the welfare system at a young age. Moving forward, I will explain those services based on my experiences with each. I find it fortunate that I have been able to provide all to children and families.

Family Reunification

In Family Reunification (FR), the children were removed from the care of their parents due to abuse or neglect. They now must engage in services with the agency to address the concerns that led to them being involved with the agency. The timeline for FR is typically between 6 to 18 months. However, if the child is under five years old, the parents can get up to 12 months to prove they have engaged in services and addressed the concerns.

By far, FR is the most challenging and rewarding. It is challenging in the sense that you may be working with parents who have a long history of substance abuse, which is exceedingly difficult for most parents. It is rewarding because you bear witness to all the hard work the parents put in to have their children back in their care.

In my experience of working with families receiving FR services, I have learned to be patient and do regular check-ins. In addition, it is beneficial to acknowledge when the parents are doing great with their services, all while encouraging them to keep pushing, even if they "messed up." It is often difficult for the parents because they are dealing with their own traumatic experiences. When parents acknowledge they are doing the best they can, that goes a long way. There are many programs they must do, including visiting with their children, attending meetings, and keeping up with all of their service providers. Coupled with taking care of themselves, the experience can become very overwhelming for them. Still, imagine how rewarding it will be for both you and them when their children are reunified with their parents, and they get to go home!

Additionally, in FR services, the Social Worker works with the parents on a Case Plan. A Case Plan is like a contract the parent signs that outlines all the services and objectives they must meet to be reunified with their children. The Case

Plan is supposed to be goal-oriented and details the benefits that the Social Worker provides to meet the family's needs. For example, an FR Case Plan would say the mother will attend her therapy sessions two times a week to work on substance abuse issues, address the concerns that brought her and her family to the attention of CPS, address past traumas, and learn coping skills for when she is triggered to revert to previous negative behaviors.

In addition, in FR services the Social Worker must update the court every six months to assess if the family is ready to be reunified. If not, then you—as the Social Worker—must explain why the family is not prepared in the court report.

After FR, once it is successful, the family will enter the next phase:

Family Maintenance

In Family Maintenance (FM), the children have either returned to their parents and FM services are offered to the family, or they were never removed from the home. In either case, FM services are provided at the start of the case due to abuse or neglect concerns. The timeline for FM services is 6 to 24 months.

In FM services, the Social Worker assesses and ensures the children are safe in their parents' home while the parents address the concerns that brought them to CPS's attention. One crucial point I always tell parents receiving FM services is this: If the agency has additional concerns and issues that continue not to be addressed, the children can be removed from their care. As the Social Worker, it is vital that you be very transparent and upfront with the families. I also let them know as soon as new concerns arise and work together to address them.

For example, let's say one of the concerns was Intimate Partner Violence. The children would not be removed from their parents' care because the parents were honest and willing to work with the agency to address that concern. In turn, the parents participated and were engaged in all the services that were offered to them. Another example might include the parents getting into a verbal argument while the children were at school. After talking with the children and doing your assessment, you learn the children were, indeed, at school and not in the home at the time of the incident. As a Social Worker, I would remind the parents about their involvement with the agency and increase their support or services.

What to do when the parents have a physical altercation in the presence of the children, leading to one of the children reaching out to the agency? It would appear the parents are not working to address their issue. That scenario may result in removal because the safety of the children is at risk.

In FM services, you are constantly assessing families, ensuring the parents address the concerns that brought them to the agency's attention. The safety of the children is the number one priority.

I have had cases when the families were receiving FM services, but I had to remove the children and offer FR services to the family. It is never easy removing children from their parents' care. I get very emotional during every removal, no matter the circumstance. One of my most memorable removals was when I had to remove a five-year-old, and he said, "Mommy, please don't let them take me." Those words will forever be stuck to me. The look on that child's face was so heartbreaking.

The best thing about FM services is that if the parents address the concerns that brought them to the agency's attention and the Social Worker had no additional concerns with the children being in their parents' care, you can close your case. That means they are done working with the agency, and you will provide additional resources to the family that they can utilize. I have had parents tell me they want me to be their Social Worker forever. However, I always remind them they do not want to be involved with CPS permanently. Nonetheless, I understand that is their way of telling me they appreciate the work I've done for them — but at the same time, I do not want to be in their lives "forever."

Just as with FR services, FM services require the Social Worker to devise a Case Plan for the parents. The Case Plan for FM services is slightly different, as it focuses on maintaining the children in their care. The vast majority of the services, objectives, and goals should have been met for the children to be in the home with their parents. For example, an FM Case Plan would state:

- The parents will engage in family therapy services to work on the family dynamic.

- They will address issues they may have within the family unit.

- They will work on communication between family members.

In FM services, the Social Worker must update the court every six months regarding the parents' progress and assess if the family is ready to be involved with the agency or if they need more time. If they need more time, then the Social Worker must explain why, which could be attributed to either completing some more of the Case Plan services or due to their still being some concerns that need to be addressed. It must be noted that the children typically remain in the home with their parents during that time.

Permanent Planning

Another service the agency offers to children, youth, and families is Permanent Planning (PP). Basically, PP is where you have children who did not reunify with their parents during the FR timeline, and the Social Worker is working on maintaining a permanent plan for the children. In that instance, the children are involved in a service called Long-

Term Foster Care. Long-Term Foster Care is when the children are with the agency until they "age out" of the foster care system at the age of twenty-one. In addition, the children can also be placed in the home of a legal guardian who is willing to provide long-term care for the children.

Legal Guardianship

As it relates to Legal Guardianship, the case can be closed — meaning the children and guardian no longer have to be involved with the agency. Before the case is completed, resources would have been provided to the legal guardian, and court documents would have been given to them regarding the youth in their care. One important thing to note about Legal Guardianship is that the parents' rights are not terminated. In this instance, the legal guardian has court documents stating the children are in their care and allows them to make educational and medical decisions concerning the children.

PP services are complicated to explain because each case is different. PP services are usually not that challenging because they are somewhat stable, and you — the Social Worker — are working to provide a more stable and sometimes permanent home for the children. In some PP cases, the children can be adopted by their legal guardian.

Adoption

In my humble opinion, adoption is the most rewarding, pleasant, heartbreaking, fulfilling, and challenging experience in the field of social work. There are countless emotions that you — as the Social Worker — may encounter.

In Adoption, the age range of children can vary from babies to youths. Although it is incredibly challenging for children to get adopted, it does happen. In Adoption, the children can be adopted by a family member, foster parent, family friend, Court-Appointed Special Advocate (CASA), or anyone with the children's best interest in providing for them a permanent home. It is gratifying to see children being adopted by a family or individual who has been fully committed to them and who will provide a stable, safe, loving, and healthy environment for the newest addition to their family.

As a Social Worker, it is heartbreaking to see another parent lose their children to someone else, especially after seeing them work hard to keep their children in their care.

There are times when adoptive parents are willing to communicate with the birth parents, which is very pleasant to see. In my experience, relatives were the ones who adopt the children in most cases, which was very fulfilling to me because I knew the children would always have a connection to their birth family. In one of my adoptive cases, the foster parent adopted the child but maintained contact with the child's grandmother — even taking the child for a weekly visit with her.

In Adoption, an Adoption Social Worker is assigned to the case a majority of the time. The Adoption Social Worker is responsible for doing all that is required for the adoption case, including:

- Providing resources to the adoptive parents by:
    - Preparing for adoption.
    - Preparing for the home-study process.
    - Providing financial assistance.
    - Assisting with any legal considerations.

Personally, I have not worked directly in the Adoption process. I have, however, worked closely with the Adoption

Social Worker to help the families submit documentation or get other things done. The timeline for Adoption varies and is largely dependent upon how soon documents are turned in and other processes. In the end, those who witness the Adoption Hearing are privy to the most pleasant, beautiful, and rewarding process.

Non-Minor Dependent

Another service the agency provides for the youths is Non-Minor Dependent (NMD). NMD youths are those who have decided to remain in the foster care system on their 18th birthday and will stay until they age out at 21 years old. The service that is provided to them is called the AB12 Extended Foster Care (EFC) program. The NMD youth may leave extended foster care and later choose to re-enter the program up to the age of twenty-one. Basically, from the time they are 18 until they age out at 21, they can come in and out of the program.

In the EFC program, the NMD youths have an NMD Social Worker with whom they work. For the NMD youths to continue to participate in the EFC program, they must meet at least one of the following criteria:

1. Working toward completion of high school or an equivalent program (e.g., GED); or
2. Be enrolled in community college, college, or a vocational education program; or
3. Be employed at least 80 hours a month; or
4. Actively participating in a program designed to assist in gaining employment; or
5. Are unable to do one of the above requirements because of a documented medical condition.

If the NMD youths are not meeting one of those criteria, they may be terminated from the EFC program, but they can always return until they are 21 years old.

Working with NMD youths can be very challenging. There are so many traumas they may have faced, and you — as the Social Worker — will be supporting them as they gradually become fully independent adults. The NMD youths choose their housing, education, employment, and leisure activities while receiving ongoing support and assistance from their social workers and other support providers when they encounter struggles. It is critical to provide as much help to them by connecting them with various service providers and ensuring they participate in one of the criteria to continue participating in the EFC program.

I love working with NMD youths. Yes, they can be challenging, but they let you know precisely what is on their mind. Some of them are not afraid to advocate for themselves, which I love. I always tell my NMD youths that if I am doing something they do not like or fail to follow up on something that we discuss, I highly encourage them to call me out on it. I give them two pieces of advice: to set boundaries and always communicate with their support system, which includes me.

There is one commonality in all the services mentioned above: The Social Worker must update the court every six months regarding the progress of the case. Honestly, the court process can be exceptionally long, tedious, and involve a lot of back-and-forth. Within the court system, you work with the judge, the child's attorney, the mother's attorney, and the father's attorney. Everyone has their assessment as to what they believe should happen with the family. Social Workers must always keep in mind that they know the family better than anyone in the court system. The reason why is because the Social Worker is the one who works directly with the family by providing services to them and meeting them on a monthly (and sometimes more than a monthly) basis. When someone needs to get information about the family, it is the Social Worker they approach.

Since we have explored what Child Welfare is and I have provided some insights into the services offered within the Child Welfare System, let's now delve into some of the pros and cons of working within the Child Welfare System as a Social Worker. Pros are the more remarkable things you experience as a Child Welfare Social Worker. In contrast, the cons (in my humble opinion) are the challenging things many Child Welfare Social Workers encounter.

The Pros

As a Child Welfare Social Worker, some of the pros include:

- The opportunity to help children, youth, and families in need while navigating the Child Welfare System.
- You are making a positive impact on their lives.

As a Child Welfare Social Worker, you have the opportunity to work with different community-based organizations and service providers that are also meeting the needs of the children, youth, and families. In child welfare, there are so many opportunities for career growth that Social Workers can explore within the system, including moving around in different departments, expanding on your skills, and adding to your resume. As a Child Welfare Social Worker, there is a potential to earn a sound and reasonable salary compared to other Social Worker careers. Being a Child Welfare Social Worker exposes you to different scenarios every day. If you are the type of person who does not like to do the same thing every day, Child Welfare is for you. No day is the same.

Other pros are dependent upon the department for which you work. As a Child Welfare Social Worker, you get to leave the office and go out into the community. There are home visits you must go to, various meetings to attend, meeting families in public, and going to schools—all while enjoying your day outside rather than being stuck inside of an office all day. That is one of my favorite elements I appreciate the most as a Child Welfare Social Worker, especially if the weather is favorable.

The medical, dental, and vision benefits are some of the most outstanding components you will receive. As well, the retirement package is truly remarkable. There are different ways you can contribute to your retirement fund. I am pleased with the way my retirement funding is set up, which is another reason I love being a Child Welfare Social Worker.

Last but not least, you have the opportunity to have flexible hours. Depending on the agency you work for, you can have flex work hours—meaning you can have a day off in mid-week. I highly recommend flex hours because it gives you what will be a much-needed break.

The Cons

In my humble opinion, the cons relate to the challenging factors when working as a Child Welfare Social Worker are that they can be mentally and emotionally draining. Some of the cases you will work on can be very sensitive and very difficult to comprehend. The number of issues you will work on and all the different tasks you need to complete per case while ensuring you are deciding the best interests of the children and family can be emotionally taxing. In addition to all the documentation you must complete and referrals you have to make for your families, you are also tasked with satisfying all your monthly home visits and finishing your case notes promptly.

There are times you may have to work long hours aside from your regular work hours to get all that you need to be completed in a timely manner, such as conducting home visits, finishing a Court Report, or attending late meetings. For some home visits, you cannot complete them until later in the evening, especially if the children do not get out of school until later and the caregivers or parents are working late. Scheduling home visits can be challenging when meeting everyone's schedule on top of your own busy schedule.

Another potential con as a Child Welfare Social Worker is that you are always writing. Depending on the department you work in, you will have to write lengthy Court Reports to update the court (the judges and attorneys) regarding the parents' progress with their Case Plan, the services the children may be receiving, and your recommendation for the case.

When writing my Court Reports, I find it helpful to have my notes in a Word document so that when it is time to write my report, I can simply copy and paste them into the various sections of the report. Another helpful tip that other Social Workers do is input the information in the Court Report as they are working on the case. Just know that time is required to work on those reports because of the amount of details that go into them.

So, you've written the Court Report and worked with the court system. What's next? The trial can be the most stressful and worrisome part of being a Child Welfare Social Worker. A trial is when one of the attorneys disagrees with the agency's recommendation, and the attorneys for all parties cannot agree. Some trials can last up to one week, where you may or may not be called to testify. When going on trial for a case you are working on, you must prepare what is called a Discovery, which are documents you provide to all the attorneys and the judge regarding all the reasonable efforts you have made on the case. Reasons for going to trial include:

- The agency is recommending termination of parental rights.
- To bypass services to parents.
- If the agency is not recommending the children be reunified with their parents at that particular time.

More than likely, you always go on trial when the Social Worker is recommending termination of parental rights and/or bypassing services to parents.

When you are going to trial, one thing to always remember is that no one in the courtroom knows the case more than you — the Social Worker. You are the one who has provided all the information that is needed, so you know precisely what has happened with the family and what needs to happen. It is all about articulating the information and answering questions that are asked of you by the attorneys. Before any trial, you meet with your County Counsel — your attorney at the agency — to prepare you for the trial and let you know what to expect.

At the beginning of my career, I used to be so nervous when I had to go to a trial. Now, I am no longer anxious about doing so because I always tell myself that I am the only one who knows the case very well in the courtroom. That frame of mind has helped me tremendously through the years.

Another aspect of being a Child Welfare Social Worker is that you may encounter dangerous situations from time to time. Social Workers often go into a home or area not fully aware of the situation or danger before them. Personally, I have not encountered any dangerous issues. When I go on my home visits, I make sure not to park too far from the house (when I can) because if something happens, my car is close by. I always look around the neighborhood before exiting my vehicle to be aware of what is happening around me. Making sure you are aware of the environment is essential. In addition, if you feel as if a parent is starting to get agitated with you and you begin to feel unsafe, leave the environment as quickly as possible by ending the visit. Always remember: Your safety is a priority of all else. You can always reach out to law enforcement if you do not feel safe going into any home.

There are other cons that come with being a Child Welfare Social Worker, including endless emails that you must read and reply to, a phone that is constantly ringing, not knowing what to expect out of any given day, scheduling supervised visits with parents and the children, and driving to unfamiliar places and areas for your home visits. There are times you may have to go somewhere that is four hours or more away (the farthest I have driven to date is four hours). Before becoming a Child Welfare Social Worker, my time on the road was very minimal. I must say that now, I do not mind going on long drives. During that time, I listen to music and podcasts, talk on the phone with family or friends (using my hands-free Bluetooth), and enjoy the time outside.

CHAPTER 2

Types of Jobs as a Child Welfare Social Worker

As mentioned previously, one of the pros of working as a Child Welfare Social Worker is that there are many growth opportunities. You do not necessarily have to stay in the same position for an extended period. In this chapter, I will outline all the different units you can work in and highlight some of the pros and cons of working in those units.

Child Abuse and Neglect Call Center

The first unit is the Child Abuse and Neglect Call Center. Depending on the county you are working in, each may have a different name for it, such as the Hotline, Access Line, and so on. Social Workers who work in the Child Abuse and Neglect Call Center answer phone calls when individuals are reporting child abuse and neglect. From that conversation, the Social Worker will need to assess if the demand meets the criteria for another Social Worker to go to the home to evaluate the situation immediately, or if the position requires a 10-day response, or if there are no legitimate concerns regarding the alleged abuse or neglect.

Since I have not worked in this department, I had to ask some of my Social Worker peers for their opinions about working the phone lines. Their feedback is appreciated.

The pros of working in the Child Abuse and Neglect Call Center include having the first contact with callers and using assessment tools and skills to determine whether the reports rise to the level of abuse and/or neglect. The Social Worker can offer supportive resources when needed. They can also do preventative work to send out referrals for the family to review the services available further. There is also a teleworking possibility with this position. The Social Worker works on safety assessment skills since all the information is only from a phone call or written report. Unlike some other positions within the agency, the Social Worker does not have to attend court and write Court Reports. In this position, the Social Worker starts and ends their day when the work is done, and they have taken that last call of the day. Rarely is there something hanging over to do the next day. The work is manageable. Since the Social Worker in this department is the first point of contact, they are the "face" of the agency.

One of the cons of working in the Child Abuse and Neglect Call Center is that the Social Worker does not directly contact or work with families. In addition, one of the other downsides is that there are not enough Social Workers to cover the varying language needs (i.e., Mandarin and Vietnamese-speaking callers). There is no resource guide or an updated list of available community services provided to the staff regularly. Other departments within the agency do not find the work of those in the call center "essential." There is no flexible schedule, flexing time, training provided, and days off need extensive planning to ensure coverage. Every minute of your day is closely watched. There is no built-in time for processing reports. Workers are constantly exposed to secondary Trauma Syndrome from the constant instances of hearing about child abuse and child fatalities. The Social Worker is restricted to their desk, sitting all day to answer the high call volume. The opportunity to travel out of town within the position's duties is null and void.

Again, the information provided is based upon input from Social Workers who have or are currently working in the Child Abuse and Neglect Call Center.

Emergency Response

Emergency Response is the position where the Social Workers are the ones to make the first contact with the families. They assess the situation to see if there is enough evidence of abuse or neglect for the children to be removed from their parents' home. If the children are allowed to remain in the house, one of three things can happen:

1. The Social Worker can develop a safety plan; or
2. The family can be referred to services from a community agency; or
3. The case can be closed due to having no concerns of abuse or neglect.

The Emergency Response Social Workers use the Safety Decision-Making (SDM) tool to assess safety and risk to determine if the risk is high, moderate, or low. The SDM also helps to determine if the children are safe at home with a safety plan or living in an unsafe environment. If the children are safe in the home, the Emergency Response Social Worker will develop a safety plan with the family. If the children are unsafe, the worker will remove the children from the home.

I have worked in Emergency Response, but only for a little while. I volunteered to help when the department was going through a crisis with having too many referrals and not enough Social Workers to go and address them. To get more accurate pros and cons, I reached out to some of my Social Worker friends currently working in that department. Following is their much-appreciated feedback:

The pros are that you may provide resources that will benefit the family in the beginning stage. There are opportunities to do overtime. The Social Worker meets with the families without having to do Case Management or working with the families long-term. The position is fast-paced. The Social Worker does not write Court Reports.

The cons are that the Social Worker may not have enough time to close out their referrals. They are always on the go. They may sometimes have doors slammed in their face. The Social Worker is the one who informs the parents they are there to remove the children from their care and home, which can be very emotional. There is often the potential for adverse interactions. You must write warrants when removals are necessary. There is constant documentation with notes, requesting police reports, and writing one's own Investigative Narrative. In some cases, the Emergency Response Social Worker may have to testify in a trial at court (a rare but potential situation).

Dependency Investigation / Court Unit

The other department I will discuss is where I presently work (at the time of this writing): The Dependency Investigation Department (some counties refer to it as the Court Unit). This is the department where Case Management services begin. The Dependency Investigation Social Worker has many responsibilities that must be done for each case. In Dependency Investigation, the Social Workers receive the instances after the Emergency Response Social Worker has determined enough evidence of abuse and neglect in the home warrants the department's attention.

In Dependency Investigation, Social Workers work with children who have either been removed from their parents' home or are still in the home. The Dependency Investigation

Social Worker conducts the comprehensive investigation of the case and prepares the family for the court's involvement. This department is where the family would have the first encounter with the court, get assigned attorneys, and have a court hearing.

When a Dependency Investigation Social Worker receives a case, the first thing that needs to be done is the filing of a petition to the court within 48 hours. That petition would address abuse and neglect concerns based on the Welfare and Institution Code (WIC) 300. After the petition is filed with the court, the Dependency Investigation Social Worker must prepare the Court Report for the first hearing, which is the Detention Hearing. That hearing happens 24 hours after the petition is filed in the court and is where the parents and children are appointed an attorney. It is also the first time the judge will address the family and discuss child abuse and neglect allegations. After the Detention Hearing, the Jurisdictional and Dispositional Hearing will be set for three weeks later.

The Jurisdictional/Dispositional Report can be very lengthy. The Dependency Investigation Social Worker must address each of the allegations in the petition by:

- Documenting the parents' statements regarding the allegations.

- Documenting any witness statements concerning the allegations. Document the children's information (if they are of age and developmentally able to speak).

- Assess the medical, developmental, educational, and mental needs of the children.

- Address supervised visits with the family if the children were removed from the parents' care.

- Discuss placement for the children, either with relatives or foster parents.

In the Jurisdictional and Dispositional Report, the Dependency Investigation Social Worker must recommend to the court which services the family would receive. Recommendations could include Family Reunification Services, Family Maintenance Services, Informal Child Welfare Services, or details concerning when the Social Worker conducted the initial investigation. In some instances, they might recommend the case be closed.

At the Jurisdictional and Dispositional Hearing, the court and other attorneys may agree with the Social Worker's recommendation or ask for a trial if they disagree. Since my time working in Dependency Investigation, in most cases, trials have been requested due to attorneys and parents not agreeing with the agency's recommendation. With trials, your County Counsel—your attorney through the agency—will prep you before the trial about what to expect.

In addition, the Dependency Investigation Social Worker is responsible for making all the appropriate referrals to the families and children that are beneficial to their needs, all while addressing the concerns that brought them to the department's attention. The Social worker is the one who puts together the initial Case Plan for the family. Before the Case Plan is developed, a Child and Family Team meeting is held to discuss the goals of the family and the services the Social Worker would recommend for the family to participate in to fulfill their Case Plan goals. Those referrals can include substance abuse, therapy, parenting classes, domestic violence support groups, and other beneficial support services. Another responsibility of the Dependency Investigation Social Worker is conducting children visits at their home or in their placement to ensure the continued safety of the children.

The pros for working as a Dependency Investigation Social Worker include not having to work a case long-term. After the Jurisdictional and Dispositional Hearing, the case is moved on to another department. Some counties have a pay differential. You collaborate with other agencies within the community to provide services for the families. You may have the opportunity to travel. There is an opportunity for overtime.

Cons for working as a Dependency Investigation Social Worker are the lengthy Jurisdictional/Dispositional Reports you have to write. You are constantly attending court hearings, almost daily. You may have to go to trial on a case. There is a lot of Case Management required. It is sometimes challenging to find the whereabouts of parents. Overall, you often feel overwhelmed with all the tasks you must complete.

Family Reunification, Family Maintenance, or Permanency Planning/Continuing Unit

Working as a Family Reunification, Family Maintenance, or Permanency Planning Social Worker depends on the county in which you work. Some counties have them as one unit, while others may have them separated. For one of the counties I previously worked for, they had them all together. That unit was called the Continuing Unit. The current county I work in has them separated into different departments.

Since Chapter 1, I have discussed what each unit does, so I will not rehash the details here. However, know that the Social Worker is also doing Case Management services in this department and they work with families long-term. The Social Workers also have to prepare Court Reports every six months to discuss each case's progress, provide appropriate referrals, set up supervised visitation with the families, and collaborate with other service providers.

There are pros and cons of having this unit together and separated. The pros are that the Social Worker gets to work with the family as they move along in the Child Welfare system. However, if the Social Workers do not switch, they get to know the family and children, advocate for them, and provide them with resources as they go on. I will also say there is a level of consistency, which I believe is especially important and beneficial for the families. The pros of having them separated are that the Social Workers can focus on one specific area, and their caseload may not be too heavy.

The cons of having this unit together are that the Social Worker will have to navigate three different services. There may be times when the worker may feel overwhelmed with the direction the cases are going. In addition, the potential is there for a change to Social Workers, so the family will not be assisted by one specific worker long-term. Case Management is a heavy workload to navigate with all of the families to which they are assigned, but they may have others they work with on a particular case who can assist with check-ins and updates. Non-Minor Dependent (NMD) or Permanency Youth Connection (PYC) Unit

If you have a passion for working with youth, working as a Non-Minor Dependent (NMD) Social Worker or with the Permanency Youth Connection (PYC) will work well for you. Since I also mentioned this department in Chapter 1, I will not go into too much detail. An NMD or PYC Social Worker works with youths ages 18 to 21, youths who are Commercially Sexually Exploited Children (CSEC), at-risk youths, and youths involved in the Juvenile System. My previous county had a different unit for children involved with Child Welfare and the Juvenile System. That unit was called the Dually-Involved Youth (DIY). The DIY Social Workers focused solely on working with the youths within the Juvenile System, their probation officer, and attended all the children's Juvenile Court hearings. I have worked with DIY and NMD/PYC youths in my career. That population is, by far, my favorite. I think working with youths is my niche within the Child Welfare system. As with anything, there are pros and cons when working with that population. For this area, I also reached out to one of my social work peers who is currently an NMD/PYC Social Worker. Their feedback was greatly appreciated.

The pros of working as an NMD/PYC Social Worker are that you can witness the youth graduate, go to college, and learn job skills. You can provide direction to the youth for their future as they demonstrate their willingness to accept your service and support. The children are better at communicating their needs, making it easier to provide support. Your work schedule is flexible. There are times when you can travel, depending on where the youth resides. As the Social Worker, you are there for the child when they have no one else, helping to provide them with independent living skills such as opening a bank account, obtaining their driver's license, and completing essential tasks.

The cons of working as an NMD/PYC Social Worker includes the potential for the youths' unwillingness to receive services. Some children are set in their ways, lack communication skills, and may have negative mindsets. The Social Worker may feel they are constantly chasing the child to ensure they are meeting all of their goals to meet the requirements to be in foster care. It isn't easy to find placement for youths because most foster care homes do not want to have youths in their home. Some of the youths' behaviors and activities might be dangerous, which may land them in the Juvenile Justice system. If the youths are not participating in the required services, the Social Worker will have to terminate their foster care case, and that might not be easy when knowing they still need assistance.

Adoption Department

Another great department to work in is the Adoption Department. Adoption is usually the department where Social Workers want to go after they have worked in other challenging units. As an Adoption Social Worker, the termination of parental rights has already taken place in court, so you are not working with the parents. The Adoption Social Worker ensures the prospective adoptive parents complete their documents so that the child or children can be adopted. Although this department is not as challenging as the others mentioned previously, there are still pros and cons when working as an Adoption Social Worker.

The pros of working as an Adoption Social Worker include not providing Case Management services to the parents, as you are only focusing on the adoption process and working solely with the prospective adoptive parents. In addition, you do not have to write lengthy Court Reports. By the time the adoptive families and children reach this phase, everyone is happy and waiting for the official word of adoption through the court.

The cons of working as an Adoption Social Worker could be you may have an adoption case drag on for more than a year or two, depending on how quickly documents are processed. You may also encounter situations where the prospective adoptive parents may change their minds. The biggest challenge for an Adoption Social Worker is finding resources for the family that will still be available post-adoption.

Placement Department

A department that is not often talked about within the Child Welfare system is the Placement Department. Social Workers employed in this area work extensively to find placements for all the children and youths within the Child Welfare system. Some counties have small Placement Departments, while others have more expansive ones. Placement Social Workers work with the assigned Social Worker to determine the best and most appropriate placement for the children or youth. The Placement Social Workers work directly with foster family agencies, licensed foster homes within the county, Short-Term Residential Therapeutic Programs (STRTP), and Resource Family Approval (RFA) homes. Placement Social Workers also attend Child and Family Team meetings that involve finding placements for the children or youths.

A pro for working as a Placement Social Worker is that you do not carry cases once a placement has been identified for the children or youths. You do not work on that case anymore. The Social Worker is not required to do any monthly contacts or home visits. Lastly, you are not associated with anything that has to do with court, so writing Court Reports and attending hearings are not required.

The cons for working as a Placement Social Worker are that, at times, it can be challenging to find placement for children or youths with severe behavioral or mental health issues. In addition, trying to find placement for sibling sets and older children can be difficult. From my experience, most foster parents want babies in their home, not older children.

Resource Family Approval Unit

The most recent department formed within the counties is the Resource Family Approval (RFA) Unit. The RFA Social Workers are responsible for approving placement homes for children. Whether it is a comparable home, a non-relative home, or a foster home, they must all go through the RFA process, which can take up to nine months, depending on how quickly documents are submitted and when the caregivers complete the RFA classes. The RFA is an extensive process that all caregivers must go through for their home to be considered fully RFA-approved. The RFA Social Worker must conduct a comprehensive psychological assessment, home environment check, and training with the caregivers.

I have never worked in the RFA Department. According to one of my Social Worker peers, the pros of working as an RFA Social Worker are: more time to support parents by providing resources on problem-solving, collaboration with service providers, a better understanding of resource parents' abilities, appropriate placements, and the ability to support the case regarding placement changes and caregiver needs.

One con of working as an RFA Social Worker is that there are fewer clinical assessments. There are multiple heavily-tasking duties within the position, including interviewing, report writing, getting information later than needed, not being involved in communications regarding the case, not being engaged in placement changes, and the limited abilities to learn new skills in the functional role.

CHAPTER 3

Organization

As a Child Welfare Social Worker, one of the most crucial factors to help you work is staying organized. I cannot stress enough the importance of developing an organizational system that works for you. Personally and professionally, being organized helps me see things more transparently while being focused on what I need to get done and helping to tackle the unexpected things that get thrown my way. When I am not organized, I miss deadlines, forget to turn in documents, and fail to enter my contact notes. There have been times when I miss Court Report deadlines as well. An essential part of a Social Worker's job is preparing Court Reports because that information is needed by the judge, attorneys, and parents. As you can see, if you miss submitting a Court Report on time, it can become a really big deal.

When I started working in the Child Welfare field, I had to develop different techniques and strategies to stay organized with all the information for my families, documents, emails, home visits, deadlines, Court Reports, assessments, resources, etc. Everybody has a different system to stay organized. Some use traditional paper organizational systems like paper files and planners, while others use digital organizational tools such as an online planner and online calendars. I have tried using the digital organizational system, but it has not worked for me. I am more of a traditional paper type of person, both personally and professionally. I must write everything down and still use paper planners. The online calendar does not work for me, as it is very confusing. I find it overly complicated to process things with that tool. Another digital organizational tool I have seen other Social Workers use is the online sticky tool. They type their to-do list on the sticky notes and put it on their desktop so that it is right there for them to see when they turn on their computer.One of the digital organizational tools I use in Microsoft is the Word software to organize my cases, contact notes, Court Reports, and referrals. All of my families have their own tab. Under that tab, I save everything concerning them as Word documents. It is essential to keep each family's information separate so that you do not mistake a file for someone else's. Another tab I create under each family folder is titled

"Reasonable Efforts." That file has a list of all the things I have done with the family that will be important for the Court Report. When writing the report, I already have a list of things that I have done and can work from that list. I also add all the referrals I have made under the family tab and highlight who the referral is for (i.e., mother, father, child). I also have a tab for contact notes that includes:

- The home visits I did for the month.
- Service providers I have talked to on the phone who gave me information about the family.
- Other phone calls I have received that are relevant to the family.

Using Microsoft Word, I have created a list of the phone numbers for different organizations and programs within the department and outside of the department. I add to the list anytime I use or learn about a new organization or program that is beneficial to me. Instead of keeping business cards, I add the organization's information to the phone list. I can also share it with my coworkers in the event they need a number for a particular program.

For my home visits, I have created a case information document, which has been extremely helpful to me. It is something I also share with my coworkers, who have also told me it has been helpful. When I transfer a case to another department, I use the case information sheet to document all the family information and referrals relative to the family. In addition, I also transfer actual court dates, collateral contacts, service providers associated with the family, and any other important notes that would be helpful to the next Social Worker. I had a supervisor reach out to me to let me know the case information document I provided was well-organized and helped her understand the following steps to take with the family.

Another digital organizational system I must use is email. Emails can be very overwhelming, as important documents and emails received could be lost. Just as I do on my computer, every family has an email folder. I also have a resource folder and another for my documentation, such as timesheets or something related to my benefits. Every time I receive an email that contains any of those categories, I automatically save them under their associated tab. If I am busy working on a Court Report and do not have the time to open an email, I make sure I at least take a moment to put it under the tab for the family to read later. That way, it helps me not to skip an email, which helps me stay organized.

Regarding my traditional organizational paper system, I have notebooks where I write everything down. When I listen to my voicemails, I used a notebook to write down the message and make a note to return the call. I also utilize my notebooks to take down any critical notes from unit meetings or phone calls. I also use my planner a lot. It is there where I write down dates when Court Reports are due to my supervisor, due to appear in court, home visit dates, any meetings I have scheduled, and my vacation dates. As previously mentioned, I do not use the Outlook calendar at all. All my planning gets written down in a planner. When I go on my home visits, I take my planner with me so that if a family has a question about their next court hearing, I can quickly tell them by referring to my planner. Important to note is that I do not show the families my planner, as it has other families' information. Confidentiality is very critical in this line of work. In addition to the notebooks and planner, I have a specific book just for my to-do list. I only use that notebook to write down everything that needs to be done. As we all know, our to-do list is never-ending. When I complete a task, I used a yellow highlighter to cross it off. The best feeling is crossing items off that list! Before I start my day, I review the list and planner to know what needs to get done and what I have scheduled for any given day.

So, as you can see, being a Child Welfare Social Worker is more than simply documenting details regarding families. We are constantly compiling other documentation related to the work. I cannot forget to mention my filing cabinets. In my cubicle, I have two filing cabinets I use to store paper documents. One cabinet is where I keep all documents related to the families. Again, each family has its own case file. At the end of each day, whatever paper documents I have gathered regarding my families go into their case folder in my filing cabinet. The other filing cabinet is where I file my resources, different sample Court Reports, and my supervision notes with my supervisor. I have also created a case file for each to help me stay organized. Some resources could be parent education classes, substance abuse programs, letters for incarcerated parents, Katie A information, consent forms, language forms, AB12 youths, therapy programs for children, and phone numbers for attorneys, parent advocate referrals, and so much more. Files help me to know where to retrieve information when needed. Also, if a coworker needs help finding a specific resource, I direct them to my resource filing cabinet. The resource cabinet grows as time goes by, and I continue to gather more resources.

I am fully aware that staying organized while juggling a high caseload can seem impossible, but I manage to do so quite well because I ensure my desk is orderly and that my stored papers are in all the right places. That way, when I come into work the following day, I am starting with a clean space and a clear mind.

Always remember to pick an organizational system that works for you and plan on expanding it as you progress in your career.

CHAPTER 4

Resources in Child Welfare

When providing resources to families, you must find beneficial resources to meet their needs. The Case Plan and associated resources align with each other. When you have developed a Case Plan with the family and have identified their needs and strengths, you will know what resources to provide.

Finding the appropriate location for services is another significant factor to consider when helping the family. For example, if a mother has to take her child to therapy and takes the bus to get there, you want to ensure you find a provider close to their home to avoid the parent struggling to get the child to treatment.

There are many available resources within the Child Welfare system for families overall, although some counties may only have limited resources available often due to the size of their population.

Housing is another valuable resource that some families need. As a Child Welfare Social Worker, if the family needs housing, you want to ensure you connect that family with resources within the area, such as ABODE Housing Services, and make sure they are associated with a Case Manager who can and will assist them. Another housing resource I have utilized is Seasons of Sharing. With that resource, they can help the family make a deposit and the first month's rent, but the family has to show proof that they can afford the ongoing housing. I have helped families complete their Seasons of Sharing application because it can get confusing and become overwhelming.

Referring families to parent education programs, substance abuse services (inpatient and outpatient), therapy, domestic violence support groups, drug testing, fatherhood groups, and other resources can become overwhelming. I ensure that I provide them with the resources they need for families unfamiliar with any of the available organizations. In the previous chapter, I mentioned having a resource organizational system and keeping resources as you accrue them. Maintaining a resource binder or file will be so helpful to you when it comes time to refer your families.

Whenever I refer a family to an agency, I document which ones I will use again and which ones I do not think were beneficial for my clients. I also ask for the family's opinion of the program to get honest feedback from someone who has used the service. In that way, I am also determining how responsible that particular agency is when I need an update regarding a family. In my current county, Social Workers can only call the "ACCESS Line" to refer families to therapy services. That agency will then connect the families to a therapy program.

There was one agency I referred all of my clients to for therapy services in my previous county. The agency was called "Parent Solutions," located in San Jose, California. They were very responsive, and I built a professional relationship with the therapists and even the director. Families I referred to that agency told me how the therapists they were assigned to were very beneficial to them and focused on their needs and the areas where they needed work.

My previous county held the classes for parent education, so all the Social Workers had to fill out a referral and attend the courses through the department as well. In my current county, we have to refer families to other agencies. When I first started, I referred clients to different agencies but have since established a professional relationship with "A Better Way." I refer all my families to that agency and am pleased to report that every time I email the contact person there, she responds to me promptly, which I value in this line of work.

One particular resource that many Social Workers overlook is referring fathers that we come into contact with to the Fatherhood program. I am unsure if all counties have that resource available to them, but both the counties I have and do work for offer that resource. When I learned my current county has that resource, I made sure to determine who the point of contact was for the program and inquired about how I can refer my fathers to them. To date, any father I have on my caseload is referred to the Fatherhood program. I believe it is very impactful, although it often gets overlooked. The fathers I have referred to the program have told me how helpful it was to connect with other fathers going through similar situations.

As always, finding the appropriate substance abuse service, whether inpatient or outpatient, is essential for the family's wellbeing. Working with families with substance abuse issues can be critical and sometimes complex because you want to make sure the problem is addressed effectively.

As a Social Worker, if you do not feel as if an agency is providing the best support to your family, you can work with the family to explore other options. At my current county, I have located a substance abuse treatment program that I will be referring my families to because I have seen how beneficial it has been to those who have gone there. I was even able to visit the program, and the staff members were helpful and supportive.

There are countless organizations available to our families. It is all about connecting them to the appropriate program to meet their needs and that is comfortable for them. As Social Workers, we can be creative with our clients and think outside the box. I once had a family whose therapy services were done through their church. The only things I needed from the therapist were their credentials and open communication with me since I had to report back to the court.

The next time you have to provide a resource to a family, ensure it aligns with the family's best interest and try your best to accommodate their needs. In addition, expand your resource binder or file by developing your resources and see if that is something the agency you work for will approve. As a Social Worker, you can introduce new resources to the agency that will meet your families' needs!

CHAPTER 5

10 Tips to Survive as a Child Welfare Social Worker

1. Practice self-care that works for you while you are at work. For me, I take time to go on walks by myself or with a coworker. Taking walks helps me get out of the office to get some outside time, helps me maintain a healthy version of myself, and helps me clear my mind. In addition, I take breaks after completing tasks, check in with other coworkers, and try not to eat lunch at my desk. I also listen to music and podcasts or watch YouTube channels while working on contact notes, Court Reports, or organizing documents.
2. Develop an organizational system that works for you. Try to avoid becoming overwhelmed with all the documentation and different tasks you must get done.

3. Keep a close track of your deadlines with Court Reports, home visits, referrals, assessments, and so on. You can do this by either utilizing your planner and writing it down or making a list of all those things and noting deadlines or the completion date.
4. Utilize supervision time and check in with your supervisor as frequently as possible. You want to make sure your supervisor knows what is going on with your families. Use that time to discuss any issues or challenges you are facing with a family. If you feel overwhelmed, communicate that to your supervisor. If you are unsure of a situation, share it with your supervisor.
5. Ask your colleagues for help. I often ask my coworkers what they think about a particular situation and show me something if I do not know how to do it. You will find that learning from your colleagues can be extremely helpful.
6. Attend training, especially if you are going for your licensing. You want to make sure you attend activities that assist with accumulating your training hours. Do not push training to the side and say you do not have enough time to incorporate

them into your busy schedule. Training help you learn more about the job, expand your resource list, and take a break from your daily requirements.

7. Take vacations and mental health days. Do not let those hours just accumulate and sit there. They are there for you to use. Even if you have no particular destination in mind, take your vacation time to get a break from the job. You can also take a mental health day when you feel overwhelmed and need a day's rest.

8. Make friends. Someone said that to me when I was just entering the Child Welfare Worker field, and I now truly understand what she meant. In this area of work, you need to connect with people who understand precisely what you are going through so that you can vent to them. For me, I have social work friends I go to all the time. Even if it had nothing to do with venting, it's incredible to have someone to laugh with to get through the day, as it can be very refreshing.

9. Do not feel you have to finish all the work or everything on your to-do list in one day or even that week. Some things will get done, while others will

not—and that's perfectly fine. Do not stress yourself with trying to accomplish something. Always remember that your mental health needs come first.

10. Last but not least, make sure you ADVOCATE for yourself. Remember: "A closed mouth doesn't get fed." If you must communicate through emails with someone to maintain a paper trail, then do just that. If you do not have a good feeling about something recommended to you, voice your opinion professionally. Do not ever do something you do not feel is right because it will come back to you. In doing this work, I have learned to advocate for myself because no one else will do it for me. Even when I work with my families, I support them because, again, no one knows them like I do—the Social Worker working with the family and their best interests at heart.

In Closing...

The purchase of this book shows that you wanted to learn more about Child Welfare Social Workers and what they do. I hope this book has helped you visualize what we do and the hard work that goes into this career choice.

In addition, I hope that if you are considering a career in this field, this book has helped you visualize what you will be doing and the help you will provide for the families in the Child Welfare system.

Lastly, I hope to see the best version of you as a Child Welfare Social Worker and thrive within the Child Welfare arena!

~ *Michaella Conteh* ~

Child Welfare Social Worker Chart

About the Author

Michaella was born and raised in West Africa, Sierra Leone, and moved to the United States of America at the age of 11. She grew up in Sierra Leone with her mother and sister and was always surrounded by families and friends. In Sierra Leone, Michaella was the child who wanted to be involved in everything and know what was going on with everyone. She always loved to help people and tried to make others happy. Perhaps that is why she chose Social Work as a career. During her childhood years in Sierra Leone, her father lived in the United States. Unfortunately, her father passed away exactly one week after she and her sister arrived in the United States. After her father passed away, she and her sister lived with different relatives whiles going to middle school, high school, and college. Michaella started working during her sophomore year in high school in retail.

After high school, Michaella went to Consumer River College in Sacramento, California, where she majored in Child Development. After community college, Michaella went to

Sacramento State University for her undergrad, where she majored in Child Development and obtained a minor in Social Work.

Michaella married the love of her life while taking a year off from college in 2012. Michaella and her husband decided to pursue their master's degree in Social Work. Michaella and her husband graduated from California State East Bay University in Hayward, California, with their master's in Social Worker (MSW) degree. Michaella concentrated on Children, Youth, and Families, while her husband focused on Mental Health.

During Michaella's college years, she worked as a Child Development teacher in different schools and Child Development programs. Michaella also worked with children with Autism. While attending college, Michaella worked two jobs while juggling full-time school and other life responsibilities. Before becoming a Social Worker, Michaella once thought of becoming a teacher but later changed her mind. Michaella wanted to be fully vested in families and felt that she could not do that as a teacher. Michaella wanted to know the whole family aspect as in her childhood days, wanting to know everything about everyone.

Michaella has worked in the Child Welfare field for about six years at the time of this writing and has been employed by two different counties. Michaella loves being a Child Welfare Social Worker. In Child Welfare, she has worked with the whole family unit, including extended families. Michaella enjoys working with service providers, foster parents, and anyone else who will support families. As a Child Welfare Social Worker, Michaella believes that families who come through the Child Welfare system need a great team of support, which Michaella tries to provide to the families. Michaella provides families, youth, and children with as much support as possible to ensure they do not feel alone while going through those processes.

Michaella's niche is the youth of the Child Welfare system. Most people say youths are challenging to work with, but Michaella views them as fun, curious, independent, intelligent, enthusiastic, and achievers. Michaella realizes that they are in the prime time of their young lives and, as a Social Worker, she will have the opportunity to impart wisdom into their lives so they can navigate life's obstacles. Michaella knows her journey as a Social Worker has just begun. She looks forward to many opportunities in the Child Welfare arena while still focusing on children, youth, and families. Michaella wants to expand on her career as a Social Worker and hopes to leave positive insights on the children, youth, and families.

As of right now, Michaella is on the road to obtaining her License as a Clinical Social Worker (LCSW) as she is looking forward to all the opportunities that lie ahead.

When Michaella is not working as a Child Welfare Social Worker, she loves spending time with her husband and her adorable daughters. Michaella also loves to spend time with extended families and friends. Michaella loves to travel, and her favorite place to visit is West Africa, Sierra Leone, her home. Michaella tries to travel home frequently because she desperately misses it. As the saying goes, "There is no place like home." Self-care for Michaella includes shopping, doing facials, organizing, hanging out with her sister and friends, and sleeping, when possible. Michaella's motto in life is, "Positive thinking leads to a positive outcome."

www.ingramcontent.com/pod-product-compliance
Lightning Source LLC
Chambersburg PA
CBHW062152100526
44589CB00014B/1807